# PERSONAL BRANDING – MARKET YOURSELF!

## Tips to sell yourself and stand out from the crowd

Written by Benjamin Fléron

Translated by Emma Lunt

Coaching 50MINUTES.com

NETWORKING

## DEVELOPING YOUR PERSONAL BRAND   1

## PERSONAL BRANDING: THE BASICS   3

Personal branding summarised

Why develop your personal branding?

Who am I? A unique product to promote

What tools for what use?

Mistakes to avoid

## TOP TIPS   18

## FAQS   22

What are the golden rules for effectively developing my personal brand?

What are the advantages of personal branding if I already have a job?

How can I be sure of creating a coherent personal brand?

What are the essential tools for building a personal brand?

What are the mistakes to avoid on social media?

What do I do if, after making a mistake, I now have a bad reputation?

## OVER TO YOU   27

## FURTHER READING   30

# DEVELOPING YOUR PERSONAL BRAND

- **Issue:** how can I stand out in the job market by building a strong digital reputation through personal branding or personal marketing?
- **Uses:** stand out from the competition, establish your reputation in your industry and increase your chances of attracting employers and potential clients.
- **Professional context:** professional relationships, human resources, marketing, career management.
- **FAQs:**
  - What are the golden rules for effectively developing my personal brand?
  - What are the advantages of personal branding if I already have a job?
  - How can I be sure of creating a coherent personal brand?
  - What are the essential tools for building a personal brand?
  - What are the mistakes to avoid on social media?
  - What do I do if, after making a mistake, I now have a bad reputation?

For any organisation wanting to carve out a place in the increasingly competitive working world, having a presence on the internet and on social media is now almost obligatory. But what about our personal reputation?

According to *CareerBuilder*, a website that specialises in job-seeking, many recruiters do some quick research on applicants by typing their name into Google. More broadly, this trend towards googling is also followed by a large number of individuals looking for a service. Whether we need a plumber or to order a pizza, our first reflex is very often to open a new internet page. Customer comments on the service delivered, consumer reviews of the quality of service, recommendations from specialists in the sector or the transparency of information thus become deciding factors when the time comes to choose a service provider.

Developing a web communication strategy to build yourself the best possible digital identity (in other words, personal branding) can thus prove to be an excellent investment. In 50 minutes, this guide will teach you all the secrets of this personal marketing so as to turn your e-reputation into a selling point.

# PERSONAL BRANDING: THE BASICS

## PERSONAL BRANDING SUMMARISED

After first appearing in 1981 in *The Battle for Your Mind* by Al Ries and Jack Trout, the concept of personal branding has been conceptualised by many specialists, including the Americans Tom Peters during the 1990s and William Aruda and Peter Montoya during the 2000s.

Personal branding, also known as 'personal marketing', involves applying communication and marketing techniques that are usually used to promote a product or company to an individual. In this way, the individual becomes their own brand. The aim of this process is to encourage potential clients or employers to enlist the services of one person and not another. What matters is therefore no longer so much the product or service offered by the person in question, but rather their reputation and their professional identity. These are created and spread primarily through the internet and its preferred communication methods, namely social networks.

But how can you become your own marketing object? What are the steps to follow in order to stand out from your competitors and make yourself attractive to prospective clients or employers? What tools are available to succeed in this undertaking? Finally, what are the mistakes that you should not make in order to avoid seeing your efforts reduced to nothing?

# WHY DEVELOP YOUR PERSONAL BRANDING?

Perhaps you are someone who does not see the use of personal branding, based on the fact that it is your services and not your personal image that must convince potential clients and employers to choose you. If this is the case for you, know that the two approaches are not incompatible. In fact, learning to emphasise your value also means learning to enhance your professional skills, products and services. The concrete advantages of personal branding should convince the most sceptical among you and reassure others that they have made the right choice:

- **Promote your activities and know-how.** What is the point of being the best in your industry if nobody knows how good you are? By creating your digital identity, you can inform the world of your existence, offer them your services and put your skills at their service.
- **Get contracts.** People looking for a specialist in your industry will call on you more if they see you as an expert in the subject, recognised by your peers and recommended by your clients. A good review, a relevant comment, an interesting article, etc. are all elements that are likely to convince consumers that you are the person for the job.
- **Facilitate the job-seeking process.** One of the first reflexes of recruiters is to search candidate's names on Google. The information, or lack thereof, that they find is just as likely to discount a CV, however attractive it is, as to draw attention to a rather ordinary candidate. Grant your e-reputation the importance and attention it deserves. In doing so, you will increase your chances

of being offered interviews, sometimes without even having to apply.

- **Grow your professional network.** Whether you are a freelancer or an employee, whether you have a job or not, developing your professional network – by networking – is essential. This network will allow you to maximise your chances of getting through a bad patch and getting more interesting opportunities. Furthermore, establishing your reputation, including with your colleagues, will make you appear more attractive to potential clients and employers.
- **Stand out from your competitors.** In a working world where competitiveness rages in almost all areas of business, it is essential to stand out from the crowd in order to avoid finding yourself lost in the crowd. Standing out from your competitors so as to make a more powerful impression and therefore to sell yourself better is precisely the aim of personal branding.
- **Get to know yourself better.** One of the main laws of marketing involves knowing the different features of a product or service to ensure that it is promoted effectively. So, if you want the strategy of your personal brand to pay off, pay attention to yourself so you can emphasise your qualities, skills and talents, as well as the underlying motivations that drive you. Before others can get to know you, you are therefore going to have to get to know yourself.

# WHO AM I? A UNIQUE PRODUCT TO PROMOTE

As we have seen, personal branding is based on the principles of corporate marketing applied to an individual. It is therefore unsurprising to call on techniques usually used in this industry to implement suitable personal marketing. As such, the SWOT analysis is one of the most effective tools in this area. But what exactly is it?

An acronym formed by the initials of *Strengths, Weaknesses, Opportunities* and *Threats*, SWOT analysis is generally used in marketing to conduct an audit of an organisation. By responding to a series of questions pertaining to each of these four areas of analysis (the specific features of the company's sector, its strengths, its areas for improvement, etc.), we can identify the organisation's strategic options.

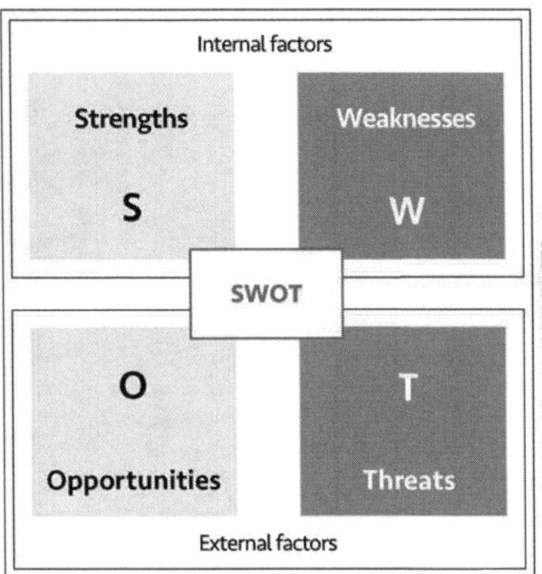



Familiarise yourself with this tool and use it to help with decision-making in order to undertake your own personalised audit. You will thus obtain answers to the following questions, which you must ask yourself in order to develop an effective and coherent personal brand:

- **What are your strengths and weaknesses?** What are your assets? What area(s) are you specialised in? What makes you stand out from other professionals in your sector? Maybe it is your experience? Or the fact that you possess a particular skill that few of your competitors have? Which personal values and which positive character traits can you build and base your personal branding on? On the contrary, what are your points for improvement? Is there a necessary qualification that you lack? Maybe you have not mastered another language, software or specific legislation that is particularly useful in your industry? Discovering your different strengths and weakness will help you to decide which skills and personal traits to promote in order to build yourself an original and immediately identifiable brand image.

- **What opportunities can you identify?** Is your line of business in the middle of big changes? Is the appearance of new technologies creating promising new job opportunities for which you are qualified? Has a skill that you possess come back into fashion, giving you the chance to make yourself known by offering training? Do not wait for opportunities to present themselves to you, but rather imagine the situation in reverse: create your own luck by starting with your abilities and ask yourself how you can make these profitable. Keep an eye on the developments and latest advances in your industry. By starting in the right place, you may be able to leave your competitors behind for good.

- **What are the threats that are likely to block your route?** Is your sector evolving rapidly, forcing you to stay on alert at the risk of becoming outdated? Perhaps, on the contrary, it is no longer evolving due to technological advances? Is there too much competition in your industry? If you feel that you can no longer move with the times in your line of business, why not refocus on a market sector that you are particularly good at? Micromarkets are often neglected by large businesses who target a broad and varied audience. Perhaps you can find what you are looking for there?



## Beyond the SWOT

As part of the development of your personal brand, it seems necessary to go beyond the SWOT analysis. Thus, ask yourself these additional questions:

- **What are your objectives?** This is the most important question as without a goal to achieve, you will have no interest in implementing a communication strategy. Do you want to land a new job? Negotiate better contracts? Develop your professional network? Make yourself more known to clientele? Once you have defined your objective, it will become your driving force during the creation of your personal branding.
- **Who are your targets?** If you are looking to get a new job, recruiters, potential employers and the people in charge of human resources are your main targets. If you wish to attract new clients and sign more contracts, it is these clients that you must focus on targeting. Finally, if you are looking to develop your professional network, the different participants in your line of work must be at the heart of your concerns.
- **How will you represent your future brand?** What do you represent? What image of yourself and of your organisation do you want to promote?

In which industry do you want to be recognised as an expert? What is your current reputation? The personal brand that you will develop depends on your answers. The first objective obviously involves differentiating yourself from others in order to make yourself seen by your target, but not at any cost. It will not do you any good to stand out if you do this by portraying values that are not in character for you. It is therefore essential to know where you come from, or in other words, the reputation that you have today, and where you are going, meaning the identity that you wish to construct and promote.

Now that you have clearly marked out your aspirations, assets and weaknesses, and what makes you unique, and you know what image you want to convey and who you want to convey it to, it is time to get started with the different social tools made available to you on the internet in order to use them wisely.

## WHAT TOOLS FOR WHAT USE?

Web 2.0 is overflowing with social media which you can use to promote your personal brand, build your digital reputation and emphasise your achievements and value propositions. These different tools, however, are not all equally useful and it is important to learn to use them correctly.

## and LinkedIn, the essentials

These social platforms are the only ones which you must be on. It is not essential to have an account on both of them: a LinkedIn profile is quite sufficient (and essential). LinkedIn and Viadeo, which are both professional social networks, are used to increase your professional visibility and to develop your book of contacts buy connecting your profile with those of other people. They can be considered as digital employment fairs. Thinking of your profile on these networks as an improved CV will save you from inappropriate mistakes. As such, only put up information that is directly linked to your professional experience or to your objectives in the area, and leave the rest for other social networks. Follow the same logic regarding people who ask to join your network: accept only those who have a connection to your career plan or your area of work.

## Facebook, between a professional page and a marketing programme

Facebook is generally thought of as the ultimate personal social network, a virtual space to relax with friends. You can nevertheless use it from a personal branding perspective by creating a professional page or by adding content to your personal page that has to do with your industry. Facebook also has the benefit of letting you implement your own advertising programme. For a fee, it will target the users who are likely to be interested by your services based on their general interests and their behaviour on the site. Nevertheless, beware of the inherent dangers of Facebook, such as photos from a party posted without your agreement by your friends, or comments that could cause damage to you. While Facebook remains the uncontested leader of social networks, it is closely followed by others, with Instagram and Twitter at the top of the list (Coëffé, 2015).

## Twitter, tool for monitoring and instantaneity

Twitter, a professional monitoring network, will be very useful for you if you want to keep in permanent contact with your industry and its players, to stay up-to-date with current affairs, to comment on them and to share your opinions. Like Facebook, Twitter allows you to promote your services through, among other things, sponsored tweets, and to then analyse how your promotional campaign is received thanks to its statistical analysis tool. More so than its major competitor, Twitter represents the network of instantaneity and of dialogue between a brand or company and its customers; it therefore demands a high degree of reactivity and continuous involvement. But, while having a Twitter account involves omnipresence on your part, this sacrifice can be very beneficial in terms of reputation, as it promotes exchange and makes users feel that the brand is thinking of them. As such, many companies have enjoyed a growth in popularity simply by interacting with their users on this network.

### JUST FOR LAUGHS

Use humour in your tweets and other publications. This universal mechanism will help you to reach as many potential clients as possible who will feel close to your brand. Nevertheless, you should avoid cynicism and black humour which are sometimes badly received by the public.

### YouTube, to share your capsule videos

YouTube, an online video hosting service, is perfectly suited not only for publishing your interviews, conferences and other filmed public events, but also to share your training and tutorials or even your films, if you are a filmmaker. Nonetheless, keep in mind that you must ensure that you post videos regularly if you want to develop an effective personal brand and build a solid community around your brand. This platform is not the most appropriate tool in this area, except for those that are passionate about video.

### Instagram, Flickr and Pinterest, or communication through images

These image-sharing networks are aimed at professional photographers who can share their work, but also at any person wanting to publish photos of their products, services or activities.

- Bought by Facebook in 2012, Instagram provides the same online publicity services as the former, and also offers functions that are new and interesting on a number of fronts. For example, organisations and advertisers can now include different icons in their promotional campaigns, aimed at facilitating exchanges. Two of these, entitled 'Sign up' and 'Learn more', enable visitors to follow the account of their choice with a single click and obtain information about the brand or company by being redirected to their website.

- Launched in 2010 by the Americans Paul Sciarra, Evan Sharp and Ben Silbermann, Pinterest blends the concept of social networking with the publication of multimedia content. It enables its users to share their areas of interest through photos, videos or illustrations. It is noticeable that the private life aspect is almost nonexistent here. You can sign up using your Facebook account if you have one.

## WordPress and Blogger, for establishing your expertise

These are the two most popular blogging platforms, as they are very easy to use and personalise according to your preferences and needs. Ideal for writing articles and sharing your opinions on subjects pertaining to your area of work, blogs undoubtedly represent the most effective social tool of Web 2.0 with a view to personal branding. Nevertheless, while they are the best possible way to display your digital identity, they are also the most restrictive, as they require a very significant investment of time.

## The site to guarantee your professional credibility

While WordPress and Blogger can be a partial substitute by offering you many interesting options in terms of design, layout and content, the creation of a personal website designed according to your expectations will guarantee you unrivalled freedom of movement. It also offers great professional credibility, as long as the navigation is fluid and comfortable and the content is of good quality. Nevertheless, keep in mind that, unlike signing up for social networks, creating a personalised website requires time and genuine technical skills. There are, of course, agencies specialised in building these sites, but using them involves significant cost. It is up to you to see if you would like and can afford such an investment.



## MISTAKES TO AVOID

- **Publishing anything and everything without considering the potential consequences.** Who has not heard of those employees who are fired for an inappropriate comment or distasteful photograph published online? Never forget that everything that you write on these medias is saved, so think twice before sharing your feelings. Of course, you should not portray yourself as bland and weak, but you must really analyse the potential professional consequences that your publications. Carefully weigh up the pros and cons before expressing your opinions online, even when, in theory, they do not seem to be linked to your area of work. Do not risk finding yourself unemployed or brushed aside by potential contracts if the price is not worth paying.

- **Lying or twisting the truth.** Exaggerations and little white lies are not rare in job interviews. This practice is strongly discouraged, however, as it is very risky, especially in the internet age. Keep in mind that everything you post will remain engraved on the internet and accessible to everyone. As such, do not make the mistake of lying about your professional experience or mentioning phantom skills, at the risk of suffering a painful backlash. Be as honest as possible in order to spare yourself a bad digital reputation which you will really struggle to get rid of.
- **Being vague about your skills and the services you offer.** Many people fall into this trap. Wanting to keep all their options open, they avoid being too specific regarding their qualifications and the services they offer, and do not claim to be specialists in anything in order to cover as many possibilities as possible. It is better to limit your offer to two or three skills sectors that you have a strong command of rather than spreading yourself too thin and risking providing a lower quality service. A prospective client will always prefer to use a genuine specialist in a sector than a jack of all trades who just about manages.
- **Wanting to see immediate results.** While we can quickly influence our digital identity by making little touch-ups here and there, the significant changes will inevitably

take more time to materialise and to produce concrete results. In fact, building an e-reputation is more of a marathon than a sprint. Building a reputation takes time and requires regular and constant investment.



- **Lacking humility.** As personal branding involves making yourself appear attractive, set out your professional achievements. An interview you did on a well-known specialised blog, photos from a conference that you hosted, an article on an award that you won, etc. are all positive elements which you can rely on to promote your image. Nonetheless, never forget that the line between genuine pride and misplaced boasting remains thin and that nobody likes self-important boasters. Therefore, do not fall into perpetual smugness, as this risks making you unlikeable to your target audience. To avoid portraying this image, consider thanking those who have helped you on your journey, without being self-depreciating, as you have created your own luck.

# TOP TIPS

- **Google yourself regularly.** Play the role of a recruiter or potential client and conduct an investigation on your profile in order to update and correct potential digital misprints that are likely to damage your reputation. Do not just check the first links shown by the search engine, but continue your investigation until you are sure that there are no damaging elements: compromising photos or photos that do not show you in your best light on Google Images, off-colour tweets with an old friend, poorly-spelt comments dating back to your teenage years, etc. Google offers professional information about you, of course, but also personal. Simply ensure that the latter does not harm your e-reputation; if it does, you must delete it immediately. Deleting information that you have published will not require much effort, provided you still have access to the account. Conversely, the situation risks becoming more complicated if the information has been posted by a third party. Ask the person concerned to delete the incriminating message themselves. As a last resort, contact Google and demand that they eliminate the compromising results from their search engine. Nonetheless, know that Google reserves the right to refuse any demand for deletion if they do not consider the information to be personal.
- **Buy a domain name with your name.** Do not wait to have clearly identified your digital identity to do this, but move into action before somebody with the same name pulls the rug from under your feet. It could not be

easier to do this: a simple internet search will guide you towards registers accredited by organisation in charge of domain name management (such as GoDaddy). These services will check the availability of the name that you wish to reserve before referring you, if necessary, to a certified agent to register. For less than £10 a year, the investment will prove to be highly profitable when you are finally ready to get started: your credibility will be reinforced and you will appear higher up in search results, thus improving your online visibility. Even if you do not want to create a website or you do not know how to develop it further, you will protect yourself from poten-tial disagreements: another professional with the same name as you may choose to position themselves on the internet, which could mislead clients and recruiters who would like to find out about you. Do not fear making a bad impression by leaving your site empty of content, as it will only appear to internet users when you want it so.



- **Do not try to be omnipresent.** You must have an online presence, but do not open an account on every social network, particularly if you are going to abandon half of them after a few weeks. Consider each of these tools in light of your area of work and the services that you offer in order to use the most appropriate ones for you. As such, a professional photographer will prefer to create an account an account on Pinterest, Tumblr or Instagram to display their pictures, while a web writer will not be interested in these sites at all, and will choose the most appropriate blog for their needs and writing talents.

- **Be active and post regularly.** If you decide to create a blog or have an account on Twitter or Facebook, plan a rate of publication depending on your free time and make sure you stick to it. There is no point posting new content every day, but make sure that your site does not seem abandoned, or your attempt might backfire on you. Moreover, do not limit yourself to your site or your personal pages. Visit your colleagues' and co-workers' blogs and get involved in their publications, comment on their articles, share their interesting tweets, etc. Not only will they certainly return the favour, but you will also indirectly make yourself known to their readers and subscribers by getting your name seen in discussions and current debates. You will thus kill two birds with one stone.
- **Pay attention to your profile picture.** Making a good first impression is already winning half the battle. Think about choosing a profile picture that shows you to your advantage and adapt it to suit your area of work: do not pose in a three-piece suit if you are looking for a job as a maintenance technician; avoid the fake poses of ID photos that make you look rigid and stern; choose an original image, showing you in the middle of working for example. Thus, a lecturer may choose a nice photo of themselves,

microphone in hand, while a supervisor would show themselves in their work clothes, hardhat glued to their head, and an architect would show themselves leaning over the desk, surrounded by plans. If necessary, consult the services of a professional photographer in order to recreate an authentic working environment.

- **Be yourself.** The aim of personal branding is to highlight what makes you different. Nobody is perfect and the people who claim to be are not the most interesting. They will even be more likely to put off potential clients, who will not put up with self-importance and conceitedness. Be loyal to yourself and your values: people will not be mistaken and you will win their trust more easily. Furthermore, in order for your identity to gain credibility, ensure it is consistent. Be authentic: it will only make you more attractive and popular.

# FAQS

## WHAT ARE THE GOLDEN RULES FOR EFFECTIVELY DEVELOPING MY PERSONAL BRAND?

In his work *Personal Branding, le moi-perso-je comme marque!* [*Personal Branding; Me, myself and I as a brand!*], Philippe Buschini, a specialist in e-reputation, identifies eight laws (taken from the ideas of Peter Montoya), divided into three steps:

| Find yourself: know yourself | |
| --- | --- |
| 1. Specialisation | Speak about just one of your strengths and don't divide yourself between several. It is better to be specialised in an industry than to just get by in many. |
| **Build your image: make yourself known** | |
| 2. Leadership | This is the 'reputation' dimension of your personal brand. It is not only about being known, but being recognised by your colleagues and those around you. |
| 3. Personality | Your personal brand must be based on your personality. Stay authentic; it is useless to try to show that you are perfect. |
| 4. Differentiation | In order for your personal branding to be effective, stand out. Clearly display your difference. |
| **Make yourself known: consolidate your reputation** | |
| 5. Visibility | In order to be known, you have to be seen. Use social networks and other tools that are available to you. |
| 6. Coherence | There must not be any difference between your personality and your brand, as your credibility depends on it. |
| 7. Persistence | Developing your brand takes time. Be patient and work on it regularly, you will reap the benefits soon. |
| 8. Kindness | In order to reach your target market, associate your brand with a value or idea that is recognised as being positive. |

## WHAT ARE THE ADVANTAGES OF PERSONAL BRANDING IF I ALREADY HAVE A JOB?

There are many benefits of personal branding whatever your professional status. During a period of economic crisis, it is particularly advantageous to maintain your professional network and your brand image, as nobody knows what the future holds. Similarly, whether you have a stable job or not, in this way you will remain open to any opportunities that may present themselves to you.

## HOW CAN I BE SURE OF CREATING A COHERENT PERSONAL BRAND?

Personal branding aims to make you appear attractive, but not in any old way. In fact, in order to be effective, your personal brand must reflect your identity and respond to your professional objectives. In order to avoid going down the wrong path, consider regularly undertaking your own personalised audit using the SWOT analysis tool. Have your aspirations and objectives changed? What has happened to your strengths and weaknesses since your last check-up? If necessary, ask those around you if they recognise you in your online communication.

## WHAT ARE THE ESSENTIAL TOOLS FOR BUILDING A PERSONAL BRAND?

The internet offers you a great number of social networks which are useful for personal branding. Nevertheless, they are not all essential. Use only those that will support your career plan. The main social networks include:

- LinkedIn/Viadeo to increase your visibility and develop your professional network;
- Twitter, which enables you to monitor the professional situation, comment on current affairs, briefly converse and stay in contact with key players in your industry;
- Facebook in order to post content in a more relaxed atmosphere, less connected with the working world;
- YouTube/Instagram/Flickr/Pinterest, which are used to publish and share multimedia content (videos, photos, drawings, etc.);
- WordPress/Blogger to write detailed articles and share opinions and points of view.

## WHAT ARE THE MISTAKES TO AVOID ON SOCIAL MEDIA?

The internet can be cruel. Indeed, while building a good reputation online require lots of time and effort as well as constant attention, it takes only a few seconds to reduce this to ash and destroy all your work. Avoid lying about your profile, your talents and your CV, as if this is revealed, your reputation will suffer. Think twice before posting information: it must always reflect a positive image for your brand.

## WHAT DO I DO IF, AFTER MAKING A MISTAKE, I NOW HAVE A BAD REPUTATION?

Unfortunately, the damage is done and you cannot undo it. Nevertheless, ensure that you do not make things worse for yourself: if you have lied about your professional experience and been found out by an attentive internet user, do not make it worse by lying again to cover yourself. If you have been a bit too violent and aggressive towards an unsatisfied client, stop now while you still have the chance. Be honest, make honourable amends and try to move on to other things. Although some people will never forgive you, a well-worded mea culpa may earn you absolution from many others. After all, who has never made a mistake?

# OVER TO YOU

You now have all the keys to transform yourself into a genuine brand that is coherent and effective, recommended by your clients, liked by your peers and employed by recruiters. So, off you go!

Use the process that we have recommended to you as inspiration to facilitate your personal branding. What you do next is up to you.

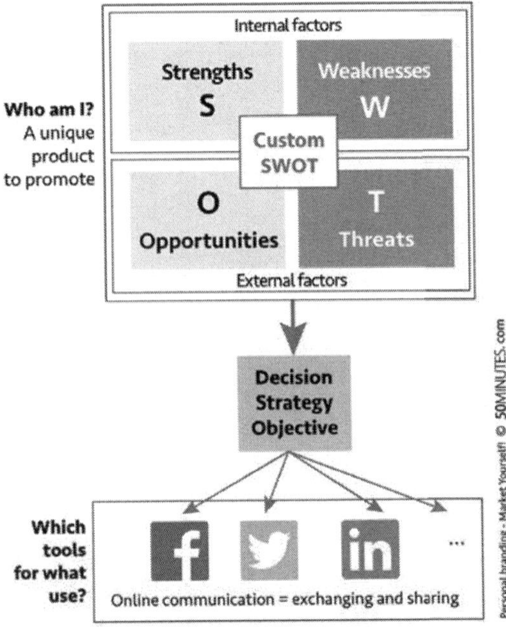

*We want to hear from you!*
*Leave a comment on your online library*
*and share your favourite books on social media!*

# FURTHER READING

## BIBLIOGRAPHY


- Bahroun, A. (2012) Personal branding: nouveau héros, nouveaux sujets. *Marketing-Professionnel.fr*. [Online]. [Accessed 5 September 2015]. Available from: <http://www.marketing-professionnel.fr/parole-expert/personal-branding-nouveaux-heros-sujets-201210.html>
- Baumeister, P. (2011) *Révéler sa veritable personnalité avec le personal branding*. Paris: Leduc.s Éditions.
- Buschini, P. (2009) *Personal Branding, le moi-perso-je comme marque!* Europe: Transition Agile.
- CareerBuilder. (2015) *Plus de la moitié des recruteurs a déjà recherché un candidate sur les médias sociaux*. [Online]. [Accessed 8 September 2015]. Available from: <http://recruteur.careerbuilder.fr/actualites/recruteurs-cherche-des-candidats-sur-les-medias-sociaux>
- Carson, E. (2014) Your LinkedIn Personal Brand: 6 Tips to Build a Strong One. *TechRepublic*. [Online]. [Accessed 25 September 2015]. Available from: <http://www.techrepublic.com/article/your-linkedin-personal-brand-6-tips-to-build-a-strong-one/>
- CCM. (2016) *Choisir un réseau social adapté à son entreprise*. [Online]. [Accessed 24 September 2015]. Available from: <http://www.commentcamarche.net/faq/40419-choisir-un-reseau-social-adapte-a-son-entreprise>
- Coëffé, T. (2015) La carte des réseaux sociaux les plus populaires. Été 2015. *Blog du modérateur*. [Online]. [Accessed 28 September 2015]. Available from: <http://www.blogdumoderateur.com/

carte-reseaux-sociaux-ete-2015/>

- Jean, M. (2012) Le Personal Branding vu par Jean-Christophe Anna. *Marketing-Professionnel.fr.* [Online]. [Accessed 5 September 2015]. Available from: <http://www.marketing-professionnel.fr/tribune-libre/personal-branding-jean-christophe-anna-201210.html>
- Patenaude, S. (2013) Développer votre réseau professionnel avec LinkedIn. *Nmediasolutions.com.* [Online]. [Accessed 8 September 2015]. Available from: <http://www.nmediasolutions.com/publications/conseils/developper-reseau-professionnel-avec-linkedin>
- Poulet, P. (2011) Renforcer son Personal Branding pour developer ses affaires avec les réseaux sociaux. *Le grand blog de la vente.* [Online]. [Accessed 8 September 2015]. Available from: <http://www.legrandblogdelavente.com/renforcer-son-personal-branding-pour-developper-ses-affaires-avec-les-reseaux-sociaux%E2%80%A6>
- Saint-Michel, S-H. (2012) Dossier Personal Branding. *Marketing-Professionnel.fr.* [Online]. [Accessed 7 September 2015]. Available from: <http://www.marketing-professionnel.fr/parole-expert/dossier-personal-branding-201210.html>
- Succès Marketing. (No date) *Analyse SWOT, outil d'audit marketing.* [Online]. [Accessed 6 September 2015]. Available from: <http://www.succes-marketing.com/management/analyse-marche/analyse-swot>
- Swift, S. (2015) 5 astuces de personal branding à adopter illico. *BusinessoFeminin.com.* [Online]. [Accessed 5 September 2015]. Available from: <http://businessofeminin.com/feature/5-astuces-de-personal-branding-a-adopter-illico/>

- Thiers, B. (2014) Personal Branding: parce que vous le valez bien! *My community manager.* [Online]. [Accessed 7 September 2015]. Available from: <http://www.mycommunitymanager.fr/personal-branding-parce-valez-bien/>
- Zara, O. (2009) *Réussir sa carrière grâce au personal branding.* Paris: Eyrolles.

## ADDITIONAL SOURCES

- Brown, R. (2016) Build Your Reputation: Grow Your Personal Brand for Career and Business Success. West Sussex: John Wiley & Sons Ltd.
- Marcoux, J. (2016) Be The Brand: The Ultimate Guide to Building Your Personal Brand. New York: CreateSpace Independent Publishing Platform.
- Patel, N. and Agius, A. (No date) The Complete Guide to Building Your Personal Brand. *Quicksprout. com.* [Online]. [Accessed 7 September 2015]. Available from: <https://www.quicksprout.com/the-complete-guide-to-building-your-personal-brand/>

# IMPROVE YOUR GENERAL KNOWLEDGE

## IN A BLINK OF AN EYE !

www.50minutes.com

Made in the USA
Monee, IL
07 July 2026